Becoming A Powerful And Effective Leader

Tips And Techniques That IT Managers Can Use In Order To Develop Leadership Skills

"Practical, proven techniques that will help you to manage your IT Manager career successfully"

Dr. Jim Anderson

Published by:
Blue Elephant Consulting
Tampa, Florida

Copyright © 2013 by Dr. Jim Anderson

All rights reserved. No part of this book may be reproduced of transmitted in any form or by any means, electronic or mechanical, including photocopying, recording or by any information storage and retrieval system without written permission of the publisher, except for inclusion of brief quotations in a review.

Printed in the United States of America

Library of Congress Control Number: 2016953223

ISBN-13: 978-1537537078

ISBN-10: 1537537075

Warning – Disclaimer

The purpose of this book is to educate and entertain. This book does not promise or guarantee that anyone following the ideas, tips, suggestions, techniques or strategies will be successful. The author, publisher and distributor(s) shall have neither liability nor responsibility to anyone with respect to any loss or damage caused, or alleged to be caused, directly or indirectly by the information contained in this book.

Recent Books By The Author

Product Management

- What Product Managers Need To Know About World-Class Product Development: How Product Managers Can Create Successful Products

- How Product Managers Can Learn To Understand Their Customers: Techniques For Product Managers To Better Understand What Their Customers Really Want

Public Speaking

- Tools Speakers Need In Order To Give The Perfect Speech: What tools to use to create your next speech so that your message will be remembered forever!

- How To Create A Speech That Will Be Remembered

CIO Skills

- CIO Secrets For Growing Innovation: Tips And Techniques For CIOs To Use In Order To Make Innovation Happen In Their IT Department

- Your Success As A CIO Depends On How Well You Communicate: Tips And Techniques For CIOs To Use In Order To Become Better Communicators

IT Manager Skills

- Save Yourself, Save Your Job – How To Manage Your IT Career: Secrets That IT Managers Can Use In Order To Have A Successful Career

- Growing Your CIO Career: How CIOs Can Work With The Entire Company In Order To Be Successful

Negotiating

- Learn How To Signal In Your Next Negotiation: How To Develop The Skill Of Effective Signaling In A Negotiation In Order To Get The Best Possible Outcome

- Learn The Skill Of Exploring In A Negotiation: How To Develop The Skill Of Exploring What Is Possible In A Negotiation In Order To Reach The Best Possible Deal

Note: See a complete list of books by Dr. Jim Anderson at the back of this book.

<u>Acknowledgements</u>

Any book like this one is the result of years of real-world work experience. In my over 25 years of working for 7 different firms, I have met countless fantastic people and I've been mentored by some truly exceptional ones. Although I've probably forgotten some of the people who made me the person that I am today, here is my attempt to finally give them the recognition that they so truly deserve:

- Thomas P. Anderson
- Art Puett
- Bobbi Marshall
- Bob Boggs

Dr. Jim Anderson

This book is dedicated to my wife Lori. None of this would have been possible without her love and support.

Thanks for the best years of my life (so far)...!

Table Of Contents

BECOMING POWERFUL AND EFFECTIVE TAKES PRACTICE 8

ABOUT THE AUTHOR 10

CHAPTER 1: IT LEADERS KNOW THAT IT'S NOT ALL ABOUT THEM 15

CHAPTER 2: IT TURNS OUT THAT PERSONAL SKILLS ARE IMPORTANT FOR IT LEADERS 18

CHAPTER 3: IT LEADERS NEED TO KNOW WHAT THEIR COMPANY'S GOALS ARE 22

CHAPTER 4: MANAGEMENT SECRETS FROM THE BILL & MELINDA GATES FOUNDATION'S GLOBAL HEALTH PRESIDENT 27

CHAPTER 5: IT LEADERS WANT TO KNOW: HOW'S YOUR IT PORTFOLIO DOING? 31

CHAPTER 6: HEY IT MANAGER, ARE YOU SENDING THE WRONG SIGNALS? 35

CHAPTER 7: IT MANAGERS NEED TO PLAY THE ROLE OF COACH IF THEY WANT TO WIN THE GAME 39

CHAPTER 8: IT MANAGERS NEED TO LEARN HOW TO AVOID A CRISIS BEFORE IT HAPPENS 43

CHAPTER 9: IT MANAGERS KNOW THAT PREPARING FOR A CRISIS IS THE KEY TO CAREER SURVIVAL 47

CHAPTER 10: 5 CHARACTERISTICS THAT ALL IT LEADERS HAVE 50

CHAPTER 11: NEW THOUGHTS ABOUT THAT VISION THING 53

CHAPTER 12: YOU CAN BE AN IT LEADER, HERE'S HOW 57

Becoming Powerful And Effective Takes Practice

When you find yourself in a leadership position, you'll want to make the most of it. This means that you want to be viewed as being both powerful and effective. In order to make this happen, you need to have a good understanding of what leadership is really all about.

One of the most important things that you'll need to understand in order to be effective is that leadership is not all about you. Rather, it's about the people that you are leading and what they are looking for from you. To lead a group of people you'll need to make sure that you have the personal skills that this kind of task requires. You'll need to use these skills to help your team make progress in implementing your company's goals.

The good news is that you don't have to make all of this up by yourself. You can observe other leaders who are being successful and then emulate what they are doing. You'll need to make sure that the signals that you are sending to the team that you are in charge of are clear and easily understood. Although there are differences between business and sports, you'll still need to play the role of a coach in order to help your team be successful.

As we are all too well aware of, on any given day a crisis can hit our part of the IT department. As an effective IT leader, you need to prepare for these events before they happen. One part of getting ready is to make sure that your entire team shares the same vision that you have for what the team is going to be able to accomplish. The good news is that this is all possible to do, you just need to master the IT leader skills that are going to allow you to make it happen.

For more information on what it takes to be a great IT manager, check out my blog, The Accidental IT Leader, at:

www.TheAccidentalITLeader.com

Good luck!

- Dr. Jim Anderson

About The Author

I must confess that I never set out to be a CIO. When I went to school, I studied Computer Science and thought that I'd get a nice job programming and that would be that. Well, at least part of that plan worked out!

My first job was working for Boeing on their F/A-18 fighter jet program. I spent my days programming fighter jet software in assembly language and I loved it. The U.S. government decided to save some money and went looking for other countries to sell this plane to. This put me into an unfamiliar role: I started to meet with foreign military officials and I ended up having to manage groups of engineers who were working on international projects.

Time moved on and so did I. I found myself working for Siemens, the big German telecommunications company. They were making phone switches and selling them to the seven U.S. phone companies. The problem was that the switches were too complicated. Customers couldn't tell the difference between one complicated phone switch from another complicated phone switch. Once again I found myself working with the sales and marketing teams to find ways to make the great technology that the engineers had developed understandable to both internal and external customers.

I've spent over 25 years working as an senior IT professional for both big companies and startups. This has given me an opportunity to learn what it takes to manage and IT department in ways that allow it to maximize its output while becoming a valuable part of the overall company.

I now live in Tampa Florida where I spend my time managing my consulting business, Blue Elephant Consulting, teaching college courses at the University of South Florida, and traveling to work with companies like yours to share the knowledge that I have about how to create and manage successful IT departments.

I'm always available to answer questions and I can be reached at:

Dr. Jim Anderson
Blue Elephant Consulting
Email: jim@BlueElephantConsulting.com
Facebook: http://goo.gl/1TVoK
Web: **www.BlueElephantConsulting.com**

"Unforgettable communication skills that will set your ideas free…"

Create IT Departments That Are Productive And A Valuable Asset To The Rest Of The Company!

Dr. Jim Anderson is available to provide training and coaching on the topics that are the most important to people who have to manage IT departments: how can I build a productive IT department (and keep it together) while at the same time providing the rest of the company with the IT services that they need?

Dr. Anderson believes that in order to both learn and remember what he says, speakers need to laugh. Each one of his speeches is full of fun and humor so that what he says "sticks" with everyone.

Dr. Anderson's CIO Skills Training Includes:

1. How to identify and attract the right type of IT workers to your IT department.
2. How to build relationships with the company's senior management in order to get the support that you need?
3. How to stay on top of changing technology and security issues so that you never get surprised?

Dr. Jim Anderson works with over 100 customers per year. To invite Dr. Anderson to work with you, contact him at:

Phone: 813-418-6970 or
Email: jim@BlueElephantConsulting.com

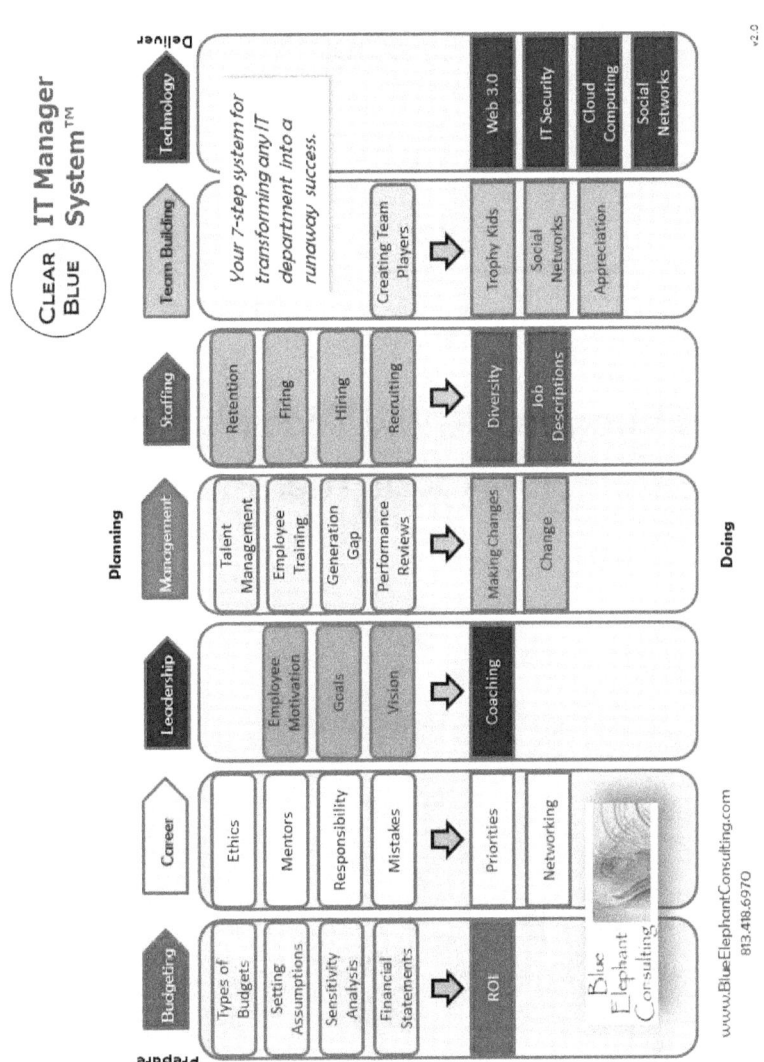

The **Clear Blue IT Manager System™** has been created to provide IT managers with a clear roadmap for how to manage an IT team. This system shows IT Managers what needs to be done and in what order to do it.

Chapter 1

IT Leaders Know That It's Not All About Them

Chapter 1: IT Leaders Know That It's Not All About Them

Please put your hand up in the air if you are a micromanager. Is your hand up – if it is then good, you have a pretty accurate picture of yourself. If it isn't , then I bet if we talked with the people that you work with, we might get a different answer. By our very nature, IT Leaders tend to be the worst kind of micromanagers.

Where does our micromanaging come from? Of course we love to know how everything operates and so we are always seeking to gather more information. This is part of it, but it's not the real root of the problem. That has to do with trust.

When you get right down to it, micromanagers simply don't trust the people who work for them. It's sorta a "give it to me, I'll just go ahead and do it myself because it's too much of an effort to make sure you do it right" sort of an approach.

It turns out that micromanaging any workers is a bad idea, but micromanaging IT workers is the worst. IT workers very quickly start to understand what is going on and they will quickly become complacent – doing only what you tell them to do and no more. This is a recipe for disaster.

So what should an IT Leader be doing? Simple, you need to be doing the following three things over and over again:

- Help your staff to learn to work by themselves. You can do this by giving them meaningful responsibilities.

- You need to facilitate the work of your staff even if you are not creating the final product.

- Finally, you should give your employees clear goals and then step back and let them work out the details.

It was the great general, General George Patton Jr, who probably said it the best: "Never tell people how to do things. Tell them what to do and they will surprise you with their ingenuity."

Chapter 2

It Turns Out That Personal Skills ARE Important For IT Leaders

Chapter 2: It Turns Out That Personal Skills ARE Important For IT Leaders

So here's an interesting question for you: in this day and age, why is it still so **easy to hack into a corporate computer system**? I mean we've had years to invest in sophisticated encryption systems and multi-step identity verification systems. The answer is surprisingly simple – the weakest link remains the people who use the systems and a smooth talking criminal always seems to be able to get the info that he / she needs out of these people.

What this realization means is that no matter how sophisticated we make security technology, it's always going to be **personal skills** that we'll be battling against. This leads to another interesting point: just exactly what personal skills do IT Leaders need to have in order to do their (non-hacking) jobs well?

IT Leaders Don't Know What They Don't Know

I can almost see you grimacing when you read the words "personal skills". Technical professionals have a tendency to poo-poo these types of discussions because we view these skills as being something **that can't be measured**. This means that we don't really value them – why bother if you can't become Cisco certified in personal skills (would that be CCPS?)

Times they are a changing and IT Leaders are going to have to change along with them. Luis Fernandez-Sanz has been taking a close look at what employers are looking for in IT Leaders and he's detected **a change in the requirements.**

This all starts by taking a look at what skills IT Leaders often **don't bring to the table.** Sure, we're skilled technical professionals, but that doesn't mean that we have all of the skills that will be needed to lead a team. Here's where we often come up short:

- Organizational abilities
- Political skills
- Public speaking
- Understanding of business language and jargon

Fernandez-Sanz has found that IT Leaders are often viewed by the rest of the company as being good at what we do – solving technical problems. However, since we often work remotely from the rest of the business, we are also viewed as needing to **improve our interpersonal skills**.

What Social Skills Do We Need To Have?

When we sit down and try to determine just exactly what skills IT Leaders need to be working to acquire, we find some good news. Fernandez-Sanz has found that the needed skills **are not unique to IT Leaders** – they are the same skills that any business professional needs to develop.

Analysis of job postings for IT jobs has revealed a wealth of data. The first discovery should come as no surprise to any of us: IT is still a rapidly developing field and **new types of jobs are constantly being created**. Additionally, IT jobs can be classified into over 250 different areas that run from software development jobs to systems engineering jobs.

Studies of IT job postings over the past 16 years has revealed that not only is IT a growing field, **it is also dynamic**. It has been noted that the languages, tools, and technologies that are called for have changed dramatically over that time. Clearly this means that by entering into the IT field we have all signed up to a lifetime of constant learning.

In the area of IT leadership, the studies have revealed the **top 5 personal skills** that IT Leaders need to have. These results have been culled from descriptions of the skill sets that CIOs are asked to have:

1. Proactive behavior
2. Team management
3. Leadership
4. Teamwork
5. Communication skills

What All Of This Means For You

As an IT Leader, you will always be expected to be working to **improve your skills**. The challenge is to determine just exactly what skills you need to be working on. The technical skills that you'll need to maintain will be constantly changing as IT moves forward.

Your real challenge will come in identifying the **personal skills** that you'll need to be able to bring to the table. Although it is much more difficult to measure these skills, they are just as if not more important than your technical skills.

It turns out that the personal skills that you need to hone are the same skills that every other business professional is working on. This won't make your task any easier, **but it certainly means that you'll be in good company!**

Chapter 3

IT Leaders Need To Know What Their Company's Goals Are

Chapter 3: IT Leaders Need To Know What Their Company's Goals Are

As an IT leader you've got a lot to do. As though it wasn't enough to stay on top of your staff keeping them happy, engaged, and productive, you are also constantly working to stay on top of all of that changing technology (can anyone say "new release"?) It turns out that you have an additional task that you might not be taking the time to do: **figuring out where your company is trying to get to**.

Why Knowing The Goals Is Important

How many of those **"corporate" emails** have arrived in your inbox this week so far? You know the ones that I'm talking about: they talk about the quarterly profits, some clever words that your CEO / COO / CFO / CIO said that got quoted in some trade journal, etc. Did you take the time to read it? Probably not – you are too busy doing real IT work.

It turns out that you should take the time to read these emails. The reason is because this is how the company is telling you where they are trying to go as a company. Sure you might be working shoveling coal down in the IT boiler room of the company, but you have a vested interest in **where the ship is sailing to** because at the very least if it hits a rock, you'll be affected too.

The leaders of your company work for the people who own the company. This means that the company has to make money or else the leaders will be replaced. How they plan on going about making that money is what you really care about. In order to hold on to their jobs, your management needs to be successful at almost any cost. **This means that their goals need to be your goals.**

How To Find Out What Your Company's Goals Are

If we can all agree that knowing what your company is trying to do is important, then we can move on to trying to answer the really big question: just how can an IT Leader go about **getting your hands on this type of information?** It turns out that it is both easy and hard to do.

The easy part of this is to **do some reading**. Depending on whether your company is a public company or is privately held, there will be either more or less written information available to you. Things like quarterly reports and annual reports, although dry at times, do make for great reading if you are an IT Leader who wants to know where your company is headed.

Now about those emails that you've been getting. Sure, any one of the corporate emails that we all get probably isn't all that important by itself. However, when you take them all together they can tell you a **very interesting story**.

Your senior management can't actually accomplish any of the goals that they set for the company by themselves. They need your help. I tend to look upon those corporate emails as **a desperate plea for assistance by management**. The tricky part is that they generally can't come out and say that their jobs depend on you helping them accomplish the company's goals, instead they have to use clever wording that hides their pleas.

What To Do With This Knowledge

Once you've done your reading, listened to any speeches that your senior management has given, and generally come to an understanding of just what the company is trying to accomplish and where they are trying to get to, the big question is **what now**?

In order to move your career forward, you need to actually **use the information** that you've uncovered. The trick here is that you need to use it in a visible way. As you work on IT projects and participate in IT meetings, you'd like to become known as the person who is always asking the question "how does this help us to reach our company goals?" Sure, it might get to be a bit redundant over time, but the word will get out that you actually know what the company is trying to do and this can be a great career booster.

Just keeping everyone else on track is not enough, you've got to do more. Specifically those high-level company goals won't exactly translate into specific IT project actions. This means that you need to step up and help to **interpret the goals into specific IT actions** that people on your team need to take. Depending on the goal, the actions may relate to reducing or avoiding costs, improving efficiency, etc.

What All Of This Means For You

We all feel that we are drowning in too much information already; however, it turns out that we still have **one additional job** that we need to be doing. The company that we work for has goals and it turns out that IT Leaders can play a big role in seeing that these goals happen.

In order to help the company, IT Leaders need to first make sure that they understand just exactly what the company's goals are. Next they need to make sure that they let everyone else know that the goals are important. Finally, within an IT Leader's team, **real actions need to be taken** in order to translate high-level company goals into specific IT tasks.

If we can view company goals as not being a bothersome distraction, and instead start to view them as a request for assistance that only we can provide, then change can happen. Your career is tied to how successful your company is and helping the company to achieve its goals is **one way to be successful**.

Chapter 4

Management Secrets From the Bill & Melinda Gates Foundation's Global Health President

Chapter 4: Management Secrets From the Bill & Melinda Gates Foundation's Global Health President

Is it possible that the challenge of managing a team of IT professionals could have anything in common with the challenge of curing global illnesses? Good management is something that we can always learn from and **healthcare has a lot of similarities with IT**: it uses highly trained workers, it's always experiencing lots of changes, and technology plays a key role in every part of how it's done. Tachi Yamada is not only a doctor, but he is also the president of the the Bill & Melinda Gates Foundation's Global Health Program. He's got some great insights that can help us do a better job of managing IT teams.

Details, Details, Details

In an interview with Adam Bryant of the New York Times, Tachi explained **how he manages people without losing control**. He explained that he tries to avoid micromanaging his staff. Instead he says that he has "microinterest".

The subtle difference here is that he is very interested in the details of what people are working on. However, **he tries very hard to not tell them what to do**.

Just like in IT, Tachi's organization has countless projects going on at the same time. **There's too much here for any one person to stay on top of**. What Tachi does is to spend time at the beginning of a project studying the various steps that it will go through. He'll identify the critical step in the project – the one that everything else depends on. That's where he'll spend his time understanding what needs to be done there because more often than not, any problems that the project has will develop in this area.

How To Connect With Your Staff

In order to manage an IT team well **you have to truly connect with that team**. Tachi points out that if you are living in a box far removed from where your team is and how they are living their lives, then you'll never be able to connect with them. Instead, you need to spend time with them and find out how they think and why they think that way. Since you don't know everything, this is a great way to learn more.

When you have an opportunity to interact with a person, Tachi says that you need to take the time to make that person feel as though in your world they are the only person who really matters. That means **turning off the cell phone and putting away the BlackBerry**.

Each person on your team will have their good features and their bad features. As an IT manager it's your job to **make the most of what you have**. Tachi says that working to bring out the good features in everyone is what a manager has to do.

One key factor that every manager has to understand is **the background of each team member**. Those on the team who moved around a lot during their childhood are generally better able to deal with change than those who grew up where they were born.

What All Of This Means For You

Nobody ever said that managing **a team of smart, bright professionals** was going to be easy. No matter if you are working in healthcare or IT this is going to be a full time job.

Tachi makes the point that to be a good manager **you need to understand what really interests you**. You need to have a good understanding of what kind of challenges you are looking for in order to be an effective manager.

Using Tachi's suggestions, IT Leaders can do a better job of **connecting with their staff** and moving the entire company forward faster.

Chapter 5

IT Leaders Want To Know: How's Your IT Portfolio Doing?

Chapter 5: IT Leaders Want To Know: How's Your IT Portfolio Doing?

As an IT Leader it can be all too easy to become focused on just what your immediate team is working on in terms of projects and goals. The problem with this is that doing this allows you to take your eyes off of what's really important: the success of the company. There's got to be a way for you to do your IT job while still **helping the overall company move forward…**

Let's Play The Investment Game

Although we live in the world of technology, we work for firms that are firmly rooted in **the world of business**. This means that they need to keep track of where their money is going. The hope is that the company spends its limited funds in a way that allows it to grow faster and do more than other firms.
IT Leaders can help the company keep track of what it has and what it is working on by creating and supporting portfolio and project management (PPM) tasks. If done correctly, this can allow the company to know what it has and then use it to achieve **its current business objectives**. This way of looking at what the various IT teams are doing is very much like **managing financial portfolios**.

How It Works

In the simplest terms, PPM allows IT Leaders to match **business needs** with the IT activities that are being undertaken to solve them. By combining multiple IT assets into a single portfolio, IT Leaders are able to understand the payback of a single project in relation to other projects that are going on at the same time. The first step in creating a PPM system requires you to group your company's assets and activities into various **portfolios**. Possible portfolios include:

- **Technology Assets:** this portfolio will include such items as your firm's business applications as well as both its hardware and data.

- **Non-financial Assets:** this portfolio contains those non-tangible assets like staff, intellectual property, and proprietary business processes.

- **Project-Level:** this portfolio is a collection of all of the IT projects that are both currently under way and those that are under consideration.

- **Enterprise Projects:** this portfolio includes all of the tools that are used within the company in order to conduct business and to remain competitive.

- **Program-Level:** this portfolio is unlike the project portfolio in that it contains the groups of projects that are related to each other – each project provides one part of a much larger solution.

- **Service Delivery:** this portfolio contains all of the non-project tasks that the company has to do in order to ensure customer satisfaction.

What All Of This Means For You

IT Leaders realize that in order for their careers to continue on an upward path, **the company as a whole has to be successful**. They have an important role to play in the company's success. One way that IT Leaders can contribute is by **grouping the company's assets and activities** into various portfolios. This allows them to be tracked and compared to each other.
A company is a business and therefore it will ultimately succeed based on how it **spends its money and the return that it can get from its investments**. IT Leaders who make it easier for the

company to determine how things are going will always be successful.

Chapter 6

Hey IT Manager, Are You Sending The Wrong Signals?

Chapter 6: Hey IT Manager, Are You Sending The Wrong Signals?

When you become an IT manager, you probably decided right there and then that you wanted to become a success. Just because you are a manager, **does not guarantee that you'll be a success** – it seems to take something else, something extra. It turns out that social signals are what determines how successful an IT manager will be. Do you know what signals you are sending out?

Welcome To The World Of "Honest Signals"

Dr. Alex Pentland at MIT has been studying **the social cues that we transmit to others**. What he's discovered is that we communicate with others using much more than words. What we are trying to communicate comes across in our gestures, expressions, and the tone that we use.

Dr. Pentland's research has gone one step further. What he's uncovered is that **we have a set of non-verbal cues**, what he calls "honest signals", that do more than just communicate from us to another person. They actually cause a change in the person that we are communicating with. In other words, what we are trying to get across "rubs off" on the person that we're interacting with.

We've all seen this before. If we encounter someone who is very excited and outgoing, then we'll become excited just by talking with them. Likewise, if we bump into someone who is having the worst day of their life, then we'll be down and glum after we talk with them.

Why Do Some IT Managers Succeed And Others Don't?

Great, so now you've just found out that as an IT Manager you are going to be **"leaking" information** through a bunch of non-verbal cues. That's a bummer, but does it really matter – I mean you've got your technical act together and you believe that you know how to manage an IT team, right?

It turns out that the non-verbal cues that you are giving off **do matter**. What the researchers have found through study is that the more successful IT managers are also the ones who are more energetic.

What this means is that the IT Managers who are going to both last in their roles and be successful **display a set of common traits**. These include talking to others more while at the same time taking the time to listen to them. More of their day is spent engaging in face-to-face discussions. They are better at working with other people and they can both pick up signals from others, get them to talk more, and get them to be more outgoing overall.

What the researchers have found is that your **attitude and the positive energy that you give off** play a key role in your eventual success. They've found that spending more face time with the people with whom you work is 2.5 times more important than gaining access to additional sources of information.

What All Of This Means For You

In order for an IT Manager to be successful, it's going to take a lot more than just having good technical knowledge. Researchers who study human dynamics have discovered what they call **"honest signals"** which can have a dramatic impact on your success.

These signals cause **changes in the people who receive them**. This means that in order to be successful as an IT Manager you need to be broadcasting the right signals. If not, then no matter how good your manager skills are, you won't be successful.

The good news is that once you know that honest signals exist and which ones are the ones that you want to be broadcasting, then **you can focus on what you are transmitting**. Awareness of the impact that you have on the people that you are managing is the key to a manager's long-term career success...

Chapter 7

IT Managers Need To Play The Role Of Coach If They Want To Win The Game

Chapter 7: IT Managers Need To Play The Role Of Coach If They Want To Win The Game

IT managers understand that they are responsible for conducting performance appraisals with their team every so often. What many IT managers don't realize is that they are also responsible for what comes next: **coaching**...

What Is Coaching And Why Do You Have To Do It?

Coaching is not managing. Instead, it's **a two-way activity** in which you work with your team member to help them improve in some very specific way.

Your coaching activities are **based on a goal** that a member of your team wants to achieve. This goal was identified during the employee's performance review; however, as their manager you realize that they are not going to be able to achieve this goal by themselves.

This is where coaching comes in. When you are engaged in coaching, you are sharing your experiences and knowledge with your employee in order to show them how they can accomplish their goal. A critical part of coaching is that **the employee must want to be coached** – you can never force someone to accept your coaching input.

The benefits of coaching when done correctly are immense. An employee's **job satisfaction and motivation can skyrocket** when they feel that they are getting personalized attention from you. Additionally, by spending the time with an employee coaching them, you may be preparing them to take on management responsibilities later on.

How Does An IT Manager Coach Their Staff?

The first step in starting to coach an employee is to take the time to **observe their actions**. The goal of doing this is to allow you to understand what strengths and weaknesses they currently have.

You should also carefully watch **how they interact with their coworkers**. Taking some of these coworkers aside and finding out what they think of the employee who will be coached can also reveal important insights.

Your next step has to be to sit down and **have a discussion with the employee**. The purpose of this discussion will be to share with them the results of your observations.

You must be careful to make sure that everything that you say is **based on what you saw**. You'll want to describe the behaviors that you saw and what their impacts were.

During this type of discussion **what you hear from the employee will be more important than what you say**. You need to work very carefully to be an active listener.

When you are an active listener you must **maintain eye contact with the employee** and repeat what they've just said in order to make sure that you hear them correctly. These types of behaviors will show the employee that you are interested in what they have to say.

During a coaching session you also have to be **asking the right questions**. By asking questions you are showing the employee that you are interested in what they have to say and want more information from them.

When you ask a question, you want to ask an open-ended question. This type of question can't be answered by a simple "yes" or "no" – it requires **a more detailed response** from your employee.

Finally, the result of any coaching session needs to be **an action plan**. This is a plan that you and the employee come up with that will allow them to achieve their goal. This type of plan does not always have to be written down, but it should be created by the employee and it should contain clear goals and a timeframe that both of you agree to.

What Does All Of This Mean For You?

Good IT managers understand that their responsibility to develop their staff includes **coaching** the team members who need extra assistance to become better. By taking the time to coach team members, IT managers can help them both improve their job performance as well as boost their job satisfaction.

In order to be an effective coach, an IT manager needs to start by taking the time to **observe what the employee is doing right** and where improvements are needed. Next discussing what needs to be done with the employee and doing a good job of listening is what will allow a plan of action to be created. Finally coaching can occur as you use the information that you've collected to offer constructive feedback.

Coaching is one of the most important tasks that you'll do as an IT manager. Take the time to study how to do it right, and you'll have **developed the skills** that you need to turn a good team into a great team.

Chapter 8

IT Managers Need To Learn How To Avoid A Crisis Before It Happens

Chapter 8: IT Managers Need To Learn How To Avoid A Crisis Before It Happens

You'd think that to be a good IT manager all that you'd have to be good at is managing people and understanding technology. Most of the time you'd be correct; however, it's the times when this isn't the case that **far too many IT managers drop the ball**.

Let's face it, **crisis happen**. We'd all like to shut our eyes and pretend that they don't, but that wouldn't be the right thing to do. Instead, what we need to do is before they happen, we need to do everything in our power to prevent them from happening in the first place. The trick is understanding how to go about doing this...

Just What Is A Crisis?

A crisis is any change that **suddenly causes a problem for you as an IT manager**. You really can't predict when they are going to happen; however, you need to be able to deal with them swiftly when they show up.

As an IT manager, **your team will look to you for direction when a crisis hits**. The decisions that you make during a crisis can either make the situation better or worse.

Although we'd all like to be able to anticipate when a crisis is going to occur, that simply is not possible. The reason that we always seem to be surprised when a crisis shows up is that there are **so many different sources of crisis**. Natural events such as winter storms, floods, lightning strikes, along with earthquakes, tornadoes, and hurricanes can all strike at almost any time. National health emergencies (bird flu anyone?) and environmental disasters (BP's Gulf of Mexico oil spill in 2010) can also occur without warning.

On top of all of these types of crisis, there are the wide variety of **man-made crisis** such as the loss of key employees, criminal acts by or against your company, etc.

You can't say for sure what's going to happen. However, what you can do is to **take steps to prepare to deal with any crisis when it shows up**. This kind of planning always pays off because the one thing that you can say about a crisis is that it will eventually arrive.

How To Avoid A Crisis

Events will happen and there is nothing that you can do to stop them. However, you do have control over whether or not **an event turns into a crisis**. What determines this is just how prepared you are – do you have a crisis plan?

If you want to be ready the next time a crisis comes knocking at your door, you are going to have to have **spent the time planning to deal with it**. That means that crisis planning is going to have to become a part of your normal planning process.

If you want to know what kind of crisis you need to be planning for, it can help to **talk to as many people as possible**. You should start with your team, but then you should talk with people in other departments and possibly even in other companies. What you are looking for is to get their wider view of the world. They may be able to see things that you can't even think of.

We often think of the big kinds of crisis, but it can be **the little internal ones** that end up getting us in the end. You need to take the time to critically look at your department and see if you can identify the weaknesses that you have. What one event could bring your department to its knees?

Finally, it's **the outside threats** that can be the scariest. These are the big ones that seem to come out of nowhere. You need to spend some time thinking about what might happen so that you can have a plan to deal with it when it does happen.

What All Of This Means For You

Changes cause crises to occur. Try as you might, no IT manager can predict what type of crises will occur or when it might happen. The best that any of us can do is to plan ahead for how best to avoid the next crises.

In order to avoid a crisis, an IT manager must take the time before the crisis occurs to **create a plan** – there won't be any time for creative thinking when a crisis is occurring. Collecting good ideas and identifying what your most probable threats are will allow you to create a good crisis plan.

An IT manager's job is to provide leadership and direction for your IT team. Just as in a marriage, **this includes both the good times and the bad times**. In order to be able to avoid crisis, you need to spend the time planning for how you would handle one if (and when) it does occur.

Chapter 9

IT Managers Know That Preparing For A Crisis Is The Key To Career Survival

Chapter 9: IT Managers Know That Preparing For A Crisis Is The Key To Career Survival

Unless you have one of those "lucky 8-balls" that we used to have when we were growing up which you could shake and it would display a message in its window ("not very likely"), then you probably don't have a good method for **predicting the future**. What you need is a plan for what your IT team needs to do when the unthinkable actually happens...

It's Time For A Brainstorm

Let's face it – you can't possibly think of everything that might happen to your team. You can think of some things, but it's going to take the input from the rest of your team in order to come up with **a complete list** of the possible crisis that you need to plan for.

The best way to go about doing this is to pull your team together into **a brainstorming session**. During this meeting allow everyone to come up with crisis scenarios and don't initially reject any of them as being too far-fetched. During this session you want to collect all possible ideas and you can sort them out later on

It Takes A Team To Manage A Crisis

When a crisis hits, your team is going to be **under a great deal of stress**. As an IT manager you need to realize this before the crisis hits and you need to come up with a plan that is going to allow them to deal with the crisis.

One way to do this is to take the time to set up **a crisis-management team** before a crisis hits. By creating teams to deal with different types of crisis (natural disaster, IT outage, company disaster, etc.) the members of your team will know their roles and therefore will know what to do.

Once assigned to a crisis-management team, your IT staff should take the time to **create a plan for dealing with the future crisis**. One piece of information that you should also be collecting is to identify any side effects of implementing your crisis plan – what could go wrong? Simply by taking the time to do this planning your team will be better situated to deal with the crisis when it comes.

What All Of This Means For You

IT managers need to take the Boy Scout motto to heart: **"Be Prepared"**. This means that although none of us can predict what the future holds for us, we can at least take the time to prepare for the next crisis.

This means working with your team to brainstorm the **possible crisis** that could strike your team. This is a good way to prevent problems before they happen. You can't be expected to do it all once a crisis hits. That's why you need to establish a crisis management team. This will help every member of your team to know their roll when a crisis hits.

Perhaps someday we'll have the ability to accurately see into the future. However, until that day comes IT managers will need to take the time to **prepare for crisis** that we know will happen someday. Those IT managers who prepare for the worst are the ones who are able to make it through to the other side.

Chapter 10

5 Characteristics That All IT Leaders Have

Chapter 10: 5 Characteristics That All IT Leaders Have

Anyone can be placed in an IT leadership position; however, what kind of skills does it take to do a good job of being an IT leader? There are a lot of IT managers out there who would like to know the answer to that question. If you are one of them, then I've got good news for you – **I know what you need and I'm ready to tell you…**

The Big Three Traits That You'll Need

The first of the **"must have" traits** of effective IT leaders is one that might not come to your mind right off the bat if you were asked to list the most important traits: caring. What this means is that as an IT leader you need to be empathetic with your team: you must feel what they feel.

That's a big one, but the next trait of an effective IT leader is even more difficult for many of us. As technical professionals we all like it when things are black & white, cut & dried. It turns out that to be an effective IT leader, you are going to have to **become comfortable with ambiguity** – not having all of the facts that you need and yet still being able to make decisions.

When faced with all of the challenges that you know will be coming your way, **you may feel like giving up**. However, if you do you won't be a true IT leader. This is because one of the key traits of an effective IT leader is that they have persistence – they just don't give up.

Two More For Good Measure

Think that that's all that you need in order to be a great IT leader? Think again. It turns out that there are **two more** critical traits that IT leaders have.

The ability to **communicate clearly** is one of them. If you have the best ideas in the world, it's not going to do anybody any good if you can't clearly let others know what you are thinking and what you want them to do.

Finally, being an effective IT leader can only be accomplished by **having the resources that you are going to need** in order to accomplish your job. This means that you are going to have to become an effective negotiator. You won't be handed everything that you need. Instead, you are going to have to be able to go out there and successfully negotiate to get it.

What All Of This Means For You

True IT leaders are made not born. This means that you can become an effective IT leader, you just need to know **what skills you'll have to have**.

It turns out that there are **5 key skills** that every effective IT leader has. These skills are: being caring, being comfortable with ambiguity, being persistent, being a good communicator, and being an effective negotiator.

All 5 of these skills can be learned. I'm not saying that it's going to be easy, but you can do it. What I can promise you is that **the results will be well worth the time and effort** that you put into developing these skills.

Chapter 11

New Thoughts About That Vision Thing

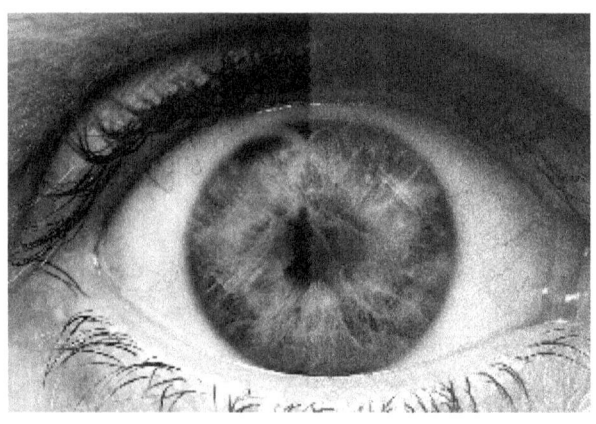

Chapter 11: New Thoughts About That Vision Thing

I'm pretty sure that your company has a vision. I'm also fairly certain that if asked, you'd be hard pressed to tell anyone just exactly **what that vision is**. Although we all basically understand that having a vision is good thing, the whole vision thing has been so badly handled that it's pretty much a joke in most IT departments. However, if you really want to accomplish things, then you're going to have to change this...

Just Exactly What Is A Vision?

So we've all spent time laughing about our company's version of a vision; however, **what is a vision really supposed to be?** For that matter, what are we supposed to do with a vision if we have one?

Unlike a "mission" which is a short-term objective, **a "vision"** is a longer term picture of a future that could be. A vision needs to be complete: we need to understand how that future would work, what it would look like, what the result of making that future a reality would be.

In order for a vision to work, it must in some way connect with the members of your team's **deep personal needs**. These needs can be based on a craving for recognition, success, knowledge, etc.

The reason that as an IT manager you want to create a vision for your team is because if you can do this correctly, then you will have found a way to tap into you team's **true commitment**. With a vision that they can believe in, your team will apply all of their creativity and extra energy as they work to turn the vision into reality.

None of us like change – it always seems to require way too much of an effort on our part. If we have a vision that we believe in, then all of a sudden that change does not seem so daunting. A powerful vision is what it takes to get us to stand up and **take action** in order to make that vision real.

How Can IT Managers Go About Creating A Vision?

Wanting to create **a compelling vision** is one thing, actually knowing how to go about doing so is a completely different thing. There are a lot of ways to do a poor job of creating a vision and you'll want to avoid them.

Instead, while creating a vision for your team you'll want to keep in mind that for a vision to be successful it must connect with your team member's deeply held personal beliefs. One thing that you must avoid in forming this connection is the use of **"buzz words"** – needless jargon will cause your vision to be rejected.

Your vision cannot be all about your team. Instead it needs to account for the larger world. Specifically, it needs to consider the needs of your department's **main stakeholders** and it needs to clearly state what the benefits for them are.

Finally, the **keep it simple rule** applies here also. The vision that you develop for your team needs to be very easy to explain to your team. They need to be able to understand it and they need to then be able to explain it to others in a way that they'll be able to understand.

What All Of This Means For You

Although poorly created and communicated visions have resulted in most IT staff thinking very little of visions and vision statements, it turns out that they really are important. Any IT manager, who wants to motivate a team and get the most out of them, needs to create and sell a compelling vision to the team.

In order to create a vision that will stand the test of time, you need to do it correctly. This means that you need to stay away from the buzz words and make sure that the vision that you create touches team members deeply. Keeping it simple will ensure that everyone on the team is able to both remember and share the vision with others.

IT managers who take the time to work with their team and create a vision that everyone can buy into will have created a powerful motivational tool. No longer will the vision be something that gets hung on the wall and forgotten. Instead, it will become a part of everyday life and you'll find that your team is living the vision that you've created for them…

Chapter 12

IT Manager Breakthroughs: The Power Of A Peer Culture

Chapter 12: You Can Be An IT Leader, Here's How...

Congratulations, you are finally an IT manager. Does that mean that you are also **an IT leader**? Turns out that the answer to that question is no. So what's the difference? Employees do what a manager tells them to do because they have to. Employees do what a leader tells them to do because they want to. Clearly we all need to find out what we need to do in order to become leaders...

What Do IT Leaders Do?

Aren't an IT manager and an IT leader really just two different words for the same person? No, they are not. A manager is able to work with a team in order to create a kind of order out of the normal chaos of life. A leader, on the other hand, is able to deal with **ambiguity, change, and opportunity** all at the same time.

Although we often associate leaders with that touchy-feely big vision stuff, it can be easy to overlook one important point. **Leaders know how to get results**. What's even more impressive is that IT leaders are able to get these results by convincing not only the people who work for them, but also large parts of the rest of the company to subscribe to their vision and work with them to make their vision a reality.

To become a leader, you need to always be aware. **Leaders move fast**. They have the ability to recognize both threats and opportunities when they see them. They use their positive energy and they pull together a response that is able to meet the challenges that they encounter.

How Do IT Leaders Do It?

Everyone wants to be an IT leader, but **very few ever make it**. One reason for this is because many people don't fully understand what it takes to be a leader.

Some people are born with many of the leader traits that are needed in order to be successful. However, the rest of us have to **find leader role models**, watch them closely and understand what set of traits we need to develop further.

IT leaders have **a set of characteristics** that allow them to fill the role of leader. These characteristics include being caring, being comfortable with not having all of the facts, being persistent, and being a good communicator. These are the skills that you can learn how to develop by finding leaders who are good at them and observing them closely.

What All Of This Means For You

As an IT manager, your ultimate goal should be **to become an IT leader**. Employees will follow and do what a leader tells them to do because they believe in the vision that the leader has laid out for them.

IT leaders get things done – **they produce real results**. However, they are able to do this by getting people who don't work for them to complete work for them simply because they believe in what the leader is trying to accomplish. IT leaders are able to make this happen because of their personal characteristics that include being caring, persistent, and good communicators.

Every IT manager can become an IT leader. What it requires is for you to locate **a good IT leader that you can emulate**. By observing closely and developing leadership skills, you can become the person who can accomplish anything.

It's from the forge of
failure that the steel of
success is formed.

Hard Work Does Not
Guarantee Success, But
Success Does Not Happen
Without Hard Work.

- Dr. Jim Anderson

Create IT Departments That Are Productive And A Valuable Asset To The Rest Of The Company !

Dr. Jim Anderson is available to provide training and coaching on the topics that are the most important to people who have to manage IT departments: how can I build a productive IT department (and keep it together) while at the same time providing the rest of the company with the IT services that they need?

Dr. Anderson believes that in order to both learn and remember what he says, speakers need to laugh. Each one of his speeches is full of fun and humor so that what he says "sticks" with everyone.

Dr. Anderson's CIO Skills Training Includes:

1. How to identify and attract the right type of IT workers to your IT department.
2. How to build relationships with the company's senior management in order to get the support that you need?
3. How to stay on top of changing technology and security issues so that you never get surprised?

Dr. Jim Anderson works with over 100 customers per year. To invite Dr. Anderson to work with you, contact him at:

Phone: 813-418-6970 or
Email: jim@BlueElephantConsulting.com

Photo Credits:

Cover - ClaraDon
https://www.flickr.com/photos/florida_photo_guy/

Chapter 1 - Quinn Dombrowski
https://www.flickr.com/photos/quinnanya/

Chapter 2 - [martin]
https://www.flickr.com/photos/mbiskoping/

Chapter 3 - .sanden.
https://www.flickr.com/photos/daphid/

Chapter 4 - Ryota Nakanishi
https://www.flickr.com/photos/129126141@N06/

Chapter 5 - 401(K) 2012
https://www.flickr.com/photos/68751915@N05/

Chapter 6 - Keith.Fulton
https://www.flickr.com/photos/fultons/

Chapter 7 - Luther College Archives
https://www.flickr.com/photos/luthercollegearchives/

Chapter 8 - Samuele Ghilardi
https://www.flickr.com/photos/samueleghilardi/

Chapter 9 - shelly-jo
https://www.flickr.com/photos/shelly-jo/

Chapter 10 - cohdra
http://morguefile.com/p/136424

Chapter 11 - wintersixfour
http://morguefile.com/p/735509

Chapter 12 - nasirkhan
http://morguefile.com/p/86729

Other Books By The Author

Product Management

- What Product Managers Need To Know About World-Class Product Development: How Product Managers Can Create Successful Products

- How Product Managers Can Learn To Understand Their Customers: Techniques For Product Managers To Better Understand What Their Customers Really Want

- Product Management Secrets: Techniques For Product Managers To Boost Product Sales And Increase Customer Satisfaction

- Product Development Lessons For Product Managers: How Product Managers Can Create Successful Products

- Customer Lessons For Product Managers: Techniques For Product Managers To Better Understand What Their Customers Really Want

- Product Failure Lessons For Product Managers: Examples Of Products That Have Failed For Product

Managers To Learn From

- Communication Skills For Product Managers: The Communication Skills That Product Managers Need To Know How To Use In Order To Have A Successful Product

- How To Have A Successful Product Manager Career: The Things That You Need To Be Doing TODAY In Order To Have A Successful Product Manager Career

- Product Manager Product Success: How to keep your product on track and make it become a success

Public Speaking

- Tools Speakers Need In Order To Give The Perfect Speech: What tools to use to create your next speech so that your message will be remembered forever!

- How To Create A Speech That Will Be Remembered

- Secrets To Organizing A Speech For Maximum Impact: How to put together a speech that will capture and hold your audience's attention

- How To Become A Better Speaker By Changing How You Speak: Change techniques that will transform a speech into a memorable event

- How To Give A Great Presentation: Presentation techniques that will transform a speech into a memorable event

- How To Rehearse In Order To Give The Perfect Speech: How to effectively rehearse your next speech to that your message be remembered forever!

- Secrets To Creating The Perfect Speech: How to create a speech that will make your message be remembered forever!

- Secrets To Organizing The Perfect Speech: How to organize the best speech of your life!

- Secrets To Planning The Perfect Speech: How to plan to give the best speech of your life

- How To Show What You Mean During A Presentation: How to use visual techniques to transform a speech into a memorable event

CIO Skills

- CIO Secrets For Growing Innovation: Tips And Techniques For CIOs To Use In Order To Make Innovation Happen In Their IT Department

- Your Success As A CIO Depends On How Well You Communicate: Tips And Techniques For CIOs To Use In Order To Become Better Communicators

- What CIOs Need To Know About Working With Partners: Techniques For CIOs To Use In Order To Be Able To Successfully Work With Partners

- Critical CIO Management Skills: Decision Making Skills That Every CIO Needs To Have In Order To Be Able To Make The Right Choices

- How CIOs Can Make Innovation Happen: Tips And Techniques For CIOs To Use In Order To Make Innovation Happen In Their IT Department

- CIO Communication Skills Secrets: Tips And Techniques For CIOs To Use In Order To Become Better Communicators

- Managing Your CIO Career: Steps That CIOs Have To Take In Order To Have A Long And Successful Career

- CIO Business Skills: How CIOs can work effectively with the rest of the company!

IT Manager Skills

- Save Yourself, Save Your Job – How To Manage Your IT Career: Secrets That IT Managers Can Use In Order To Have A Successful Career

- Growing Your CIO Career: How CIOs Can Work With The Entire Company In Order To Be Successful

- How IT Managers Can Make Innovation Happen: Tips And Techniques For IT Managers To Use In Order To Make Innovation Happen In Their Teams

- Staffing Skills IT Managers Must Have: Tips And Techniques That IT Managers Can Use In Order To Correctly Staff Their Teams

- Secrets Of Effective Leadership For IT Managers: Tips And Techniques That IT Managers Can Use In Order To Develop Leadership Skills

- IT Manager Career Secrets: Tips And Techniques That IT Managers Can Use In Order To Have A Successful Career

- IT Manager Budgeting Skills: How IT Managers Can Request, Manage, Use, And Track Their Funding

- Secrets Of Managing Budgets: What IT Managers Need To Know In Order To Understand How Their Company Uses Money

Negotiating

- Learn How To Signal In Your Next Negotiation: How To Develop The Skill Of Effective Signaling In A Negotiation In Order To Get The Best Possible Outcome

- Learn The Skill Of Exploring In A Negotiation: How To Develop The Skill Of Exploring What Is Possible In A Negotiation In Order To Reach The Best Possible Deal

- Learn How To Argue In Your Next Negotiation: How To Develop The Skill Of Effective Arguing In A Negotiation In Order To Get The Best Possible Outcome|

- How To Open Your Next Negotiation: How To Start A Negotiation In Order To Get The Best Possible Outcome

- Preparing For Your Next Negotiation: What You Need To Do BEFORE A Negotiation Starts In Order To Get The Best Possible Deal

- Learn How To Package Trades In Your Next Negotiation

- All Good Things Come To An End: How To Close A Negotiation - How To Develop The Skill Of Closing In Order To Get The Best Possible Outcome From A Negotiation

Miscellaneous

- The Internet-Enabled Successful School District Superintendent: How To Use The Internet To Boost Parental Involvement In Your Schools

- Power Distribution Unit (PDU) Secrets: What Everyone Who Works In A Data Center Needs To Know!

- Making The Jump: How To Land Your Dream Job When You Get Out Of College!

- How To Use The Internet To Create Successful Students And Involved Parents

"Tips And Techniques That IT Managers Can Use In Order To Develop Leadership Skills"

> This book has been written with one goal in mind – to show you how an IT manager can build needed leadership skills. It's not easy being an IT manager so we're going to show you what you need to be doing in order to not only manage your team, but to also be a leader to them!
>
> **Let's Make Your IT Career A Success!**

What You'll Find Inside:

- **IT TURNS OUT THAT PERSONAL SKILLS ARE IMPORTANT FOR IT LEADERS**

- **MANAGEMENT SECRETS FROM THE BILL & MELINDA GATES FOUNDATION'S GLOBAL HEALTH PRESIDENT**

- **HEY IT MANAGER, ARE YOU SENDING THE WRONG SIGNALS?**

- **IT MANAGERS NEED TO LEARN HOW TO AVOID A CRISIS BEFORE IT HAPPENS**

Dr. Jim Anderson brings his 25 years of real-world experience to this book. He's been an IT manager at some of the world's largest firms. He's going to show you what you need to do (and not do!) in order to successfully manage your career!

www.ingramcontent.com/pod-product-compliance
Lightning Source LLC
Chambersburg PA
CBHW060418190526
45169CB00002B/949